A RIGHT OLI

Bethie Jayne

Table of Contents

Foreword

Some people watch life. Some people see it. Bethie is one of the latter. They see life in a way that captures those nuances, those emotions and those mannerisms that define people. I had the privilege to work with the author. An excellent teacher of English (and strict librarian!) the author was never without their notebook. Bethie would be drafting new verses about colleagues and incidents throughout the day. Within moments of reading them I could recognise exactly whom or what the subject of each poem was.

The clarity was not the skill. The real skill was ability to stick to the facts and avoid caricature. The genius is that this is true for the places and the experiences described by the author. The result is 'A Right Old Mix' of poems and prose crafted in a variety of styles.

All come from author's heart. We dip into Bethie's journey, sharing their experiences at key points. Lapping seas, bustling town centres, joy and betrayal are all there. Sometimes these are raw emotions, occassionally uncomfortable. We share those emotions because they are written in a way we can understand them. They are relatable through the honesty of what is written on the page.

'A Right Old Mix' is one of those rare titles that captures both the content and the author. Bethie is the cleverest person I have met: bilingual, a psychologist, a poet (although don't think that's the extent of AROM) and lover of countless TV series. Like many amazing people the author suffers from a modest streak. Let us all be grateful that they feel confident to let us share their journey through life and maybe better understand our own.

Dr Chris Chilcott

Historian & Author

PLACES

Flying

A sea of clouds,
No land in sight,
Watery blue sky,
A wonder of flights,

High up in the atmosphere,
Relaxing sensation,
The gentle bank smoothly done,
Hot destination the motivation,

Different shapes,
Different shades,
A marvel to behold,
An image to retain,

High in the sky,
Your worries all gone,
Fly with your imagination,
Ages before the flights done,

A sinking sensation,
Pulls you out of the clouds,
A bump jolts you awake,
Down on Earth once again,
Reality resumes its original shape.

The Train Station

Daytime trains will stop and start,
Some will just pass on through,
Mainly on time, though when they aren't,
The heart starts to flutter as if on cue,

The station though, never varies,
People everywhere with bags and cases,
The porters run around like fairies,
Barely registering anyone's faces,

At night it is quite a different story,
As the cold sweeps in,
Bathed in soft light, in all its glory,
The perfect playground for sin,

Early morning, just before dawn,
Commuters appear like ghostly figures,
Rushing around like new-born fawn,
Yet as nervous as first-time grave diggers,

Once dawn is approached,
Out come the fairies to dance and sing,
Rejoicing at the sound of a coach,
Bringing the people, all chattering, in,
Like the sound of a spring,
And everything starts all over again,
Many of whom think it's a real pain!

The Beach

Sea swells gently lapping the shore,
Sea gulls lazily circling above,
Children shrieking in delight,
That's what the beach is for,

Fishing boats out at sea,
Dogs splashing in and out of the waves,
The cool sand soothing underfoot,
A breeze hugs you in the heat of day,

People's chatter, runaway brollies,
Kids playing football under clear blue skies,
A picture-perfect afternoon,
As an elderly couple splash by,

Suddenly the breeze picks up,
Grey clouds fill the sky,
Boats cover the horizon end to end,
It's turning cold as shadows lengthen,

People run around gathering their things,
As rain starts to gently fall,
The sea suddenly turns angry,
Due to the arrival of a white squall.

Surrey Forests

Shrouded in mist,
Lost in time,
Tales of the past,
Set down in rhymes,
Heavy with history,
Hiding secrets well,
Rolling over the slopes,
Never to tell,
Gently mocking us,
Laughing inwardly,
As we struggle for answers,
So afraid, cowardly,
Forever in time,
Its secrets it will keep,
Deeply hidden,
In an eternal sleep,
Of the deepest green,
And tallest tress,
Dark and foreboding,
Are the roads of Surrey,
Darker still are the hidden paths,
That through the forest wind,
Taunting and teasing,
So hard to find.

Mountains

Watching as the seasons change,
Giving the mountains new life,
Solid yet forever changing,
They watch as we struggle with strife,

Silently they stand,
Proud and tall,
Reminding us that they,
Are the wisest of us all,

Constantly we struggle,
With never-ending battles,
Always rounded up and counted,
Like a herd of cattle,

Yet every battle we face,
The mountains stand strong,
The image of solidarity,
To be passed around the throng,

They have lived through the ages,
They will stand, still after we are gone,
Silent and Strong, Tall and Proud,
They will sing to themselves, of all,
Our deeds, our failures, our heroism,
Until they too are covered,
By Time's soft shroud.

Autumn Starts

The gravel crunches underfoot,
Glittering like diamonds,
The cat, black as soot,
Streaks across the grounds,

The grass shimmers brightly,
Underneath the pale moonlight,
The sky, suddenly sparkly,
As the clouds say goodnight,

The freshly wet wood,
Stands tall and proud,
As beneath nights velvet hood,
It listens to the night-time crowd,

The first true rainfall,
To mark the changing season,
As migrating birds call,
Their departure seeming like treason,

The gardens bare of summer song,
As the birds take flight,
Winter ere seems ever long,
Summer far beyond our sight.

Road Trip

The heat snakes its way,
Across the winding road,
As the sun has her say,
In the striking sapphire sky,

The land always changing,
North all the way South,
As the clouds are making,
Their way slowly to Rivers mouth,

Village after Village, Town after Town,
We gradually pass through,
As we make our way slowing down,
The long and snakelike road,

Finally, we arrive,
Bend after tiring bend,
Here we are at last,
Our journey's end.

The Other Side

The other side of make-believe,
The other world is comforting,
The escape everybody longs for,
The place where nothing stings,

Reality bites, often and hard,
Causing no end of stress and pain,
The fantasy is what we all look for,
A world, though, where there is no gain,

Reality sucks but it is life,
Struggle is part of growing,
Without it we learn nothing,
With Reality we continue evolving,

Fantasy is good for a while,
Fantasy gives us a nice break,
But soon Reality strikes again,
Fantasy, though comforting, is Fake,

Fake is never worth anything,
Reality is what gives us strength,
Fantasy allows us to recharge,
So, in life, we can go to any lengths.

A Spanish Beach Café

The sun scorches,
The sea is flat,
The breeze ripples,
As I lie on my back,
The voices float up,
From the sand below,
Many of whom,
Have yet to know,
Just what the summer,
Truly can mean,
Real Spanish treats,
That are yet to be seen,
The breeze picks up,
As I sit in the shade,
Relaxing at the café,
Happy to just sit and gaze,
Out over the horizon,
Listening to the waves,
Not really seeing,
Anything through the heat haze,
My mind begins to wander,
As the heat seeps in,
I continue to stare yonder,
As the light begins to dim,
Lost in my world of fantasy,
Living a dream,
That no one else can see,
Where nothing is as it seems.

Kestral

As the sun climbs high into the azure sky,
A nearby flutter of wings catch my eye,
I turn to look and see an image of beauty,
Stun me into silence and stupidity,

A creature of quartz colour and hue,
Rises up out of the field into the blue,
Silently it ascends higher and higher,
And begins to lazily circle and admire,

Rising with pockets of thermal air,
It glides up and over a small hill,
Flexes its wings and circles round again,
Ever searching the horizon and plains.

Middle of town Christmas shopping

Christmas comes but once a year,
People become stampeding herds,
Gearing up for the seasonal cheer,
That beats the sound of singing birds,
All across the entire planet,
Preparations are in full swing,
Objects fly off the shelves like gannets,
Ready for their summer fling,
When at last the Day has dawned,
Magic sweetly fills the air,
From fending off a sleepy yawn,
To snoozing in the evening chair,
Satisfaction reigns supreme,
As everything is done to extremes.

PERSONAL

A Repetition of Fear

Sitting in bed, wide awake,
The sounds of the night comforting,
Surrounding me like a soft blanket,
My mind too active to sleep,
Once again things are wrong,
Once again stress takes over,
Still I find I must be strong,
To carry on as I should,
It is still far from easy,
Attested by the fact I´m still awake,
As usual feeling incredibly queasy,
At the thought of what tomorrow will bring,
No doubt it´ll be the same as always,
Screaming, shouting frustration and despair,
Everyone seeing through the same angry haze,
Old feelings that we have to share,
Nothing in this house is changing,
I fear what lies ahead again,
The past memories of happiness are fading,
Leaving only the memories of pain,
How to survive such an onslaught?
How to pull through such agony?
Scars left from so many battles fought,
Yet completely blinded by pain,
So self-righteous, so self-absorbed,
Completely oblivious to everyone else,
Everything not wanted becomes a chore,
Not wanting to know invites Irrationality,

Constantly assaulted by conflicting feelings,
How does one learn to separate?
In all awkward dealings,
The same arguments that always arise,
Many nights have led to lack of sleep,
Many days have been a trial,
Immersed in this incredibly deep,
How can we ever find our feet?
Stressful? Unbelievably so,
Can this really continue this way?
Fearful, trapped, as bewildered as a doe,
Which way are we supposed to go?
When, finally, we get a respite,
We still can´t relax,
Always watching, waiting, out of sight,
We know is the next attack,
Why can´t we shake this terrible cycle?
How hard is it to let go?
Let go and soar like an Eagle,
High above these petty emotions and co,
Yet, for some reason, we stay grounded,
Stuck in a vicious, vice-like grip,
Consistently and fervently assaulted,
By the same, ever living emotions,
A new day, a new dawn,
Brings about nothing but dread,
New creatures are being born,
Yet we remain constantly torn,
Never, it seems, to move on ahead.

Temper

Fire flows through the forest,
As fervently as a rampaging river,
Roaring away obliviously,
Leaving devastation in its wake,

A fire burns continuously,
Every day it burns anew,
Behaving more despicably,
Respites there are but few,

How to dampen its rampage?
How to see?
This cannot continue over the page,
It has GOT to cease,

When will it burn out?
When will it cool down?
When can we talk rationally?
How long for this time to come around?

Is there any way for it to stop?
Or has it burnt for too long?
Can we become what we are not?
Or has that chance long gone?

Fire cannot be trusted, Fire cannot be tamed,
No wonder we are so burnt,
Wreathed forever in hot flames.

Ups and downs

Forging a new life for oneself,
Is never as easy as it seems,
Everything continually fluctuates,
As constant as a babbling stream,

Tantalizingly everything hovers,
Always just within my grasp,
Then it runs and hides under cover,
Like everything else in my past,

Bright blue skies and searing sun,
Give me continual strength to see,
Help me to carry on,
Become who I'm supposed to be,

Walking tall and feeling great,
Then something gets in the way,
Something slams on the brakes,
Everything in my world turns grey,

Cold and wet and dull and grey,
Is how I awaken,
To find a brand-new day,
Bad feelings not yet shaken,

The sight out the window,
Doesn't improve my mood,
Everywhere full of shadows,
All I can think of is food,

I leave the room in low spirits,
As I reach my destination, Thunder strikes,
Lightning flashes suddenly, I fear it,
Then I feel the fire, a reason to fight,

I let go, on my ground I stood,
The battles done,
I've had my say and,
Now I feel quite good.

Dance

I'm flying through the air,
My feet don't touch the ground,
I can feel everybody's stare,
Following me like hounds,

I'm not aware,
I only move,
I really don't care,
I'm in the groove,

I only hear the beat,
I only feel my partners hands,
I just move my feet,
And listen to the band,

I'm riding on a cloud,
The music the only sound,
A blur is how I see the crowd,
The stage is my playground,

Guided by my partner,
Blindly following him,
Glad I don't hear laughter,
Just listening to him softly sing,

Feeling light as a feather, No true sensations,
Dancing is my treasure, Never any hesitation.

Response For A Bully

You have no idea,
What's happened in my life,
Yet you have no hesitation,
Throwing words which cut like a knife,
How can you be so blind?
How is it you cannot see?
Everyone is different,
Including little old me,
So instead of standing there,
And judging me with a frown,
How about getting to know me?
Instead of putting me down?
You may be pleasantly surprised,
We may be more alike than you think,
You will never know though,
As your ship will be the one to sink,
I will hold my head up high,
As you drown in regret and sorrow,
I will be the one with the clear conscious,
I will be the one to sail through tomorrow.

Unbelievable

As a new day dawns,
The fireworks start,
Before we've even had breakfast,
The air is filled with sparks,
They rain down relentlessly,
Burning everything as they go,
Stopping them is fruitless,
The One who sends them will never know,
Just how much we are in pain,
How much we are suffering,
What we really wish for,
A day without arguing,
Will we ever get one?
Something tells me not,
We are destined to continue,
In this ever-boiling pot.

Let Down

Expectations were high,
Thoughts were happy,
Plans made with contented sighs,
The future looked bright,
Gradually that light dimmed,
Plans fell through one by one,
Thoughts turned darker,
The future no longer fun,
So many things were said,
The opposite was done,
All that's left is my bed,
To hide away from the sun,
You promised so much,
And failed to deliver,
Gave me things to clutch,
Made me believe you're a giver,
But now it's empty days and thoughts,
Pain and regret are the game that you play,
Left me tied up in emotional knots,
Feeling nothing except shame,
Shame for trusting you,
Shame for letting you play me,
Shame for daring to believe,
That maybe, I could finally be free.

Shade

Feeling cornered, hemmed in,
No escape, cannot breathe,
Everything black as night,
No light to help me see,

Which way do I turn?
Where do I go? Lost, so lost,
All alone in this fight,
No paths ever crossed,

No guide, no clues,
No help, on my own,
Always alone to face it all,
Equal opportunities all but flown,

Nothing but stress every day,
This modern world is Hell,
Cold, uncaring, and numb to all,
Scars so deep none can tell,

Just how damaged I really am,
The abuse continues day by day,
Kicked all the time I am down,
Never getting a say,

Boundaries completely ignored,
My voice never heard,
What I want doesn't matter,
I cannot voice a single word,
No energy, no emotion,
I have nothing left,
Why should I bother for others?
When I am always left bereft?

I am a person same as everyone,
I matter too, yet I am invisible,
Needed for the necessity of others,
My time apparently divisible,

Do everything for everyone else,
I don't matter because I am not seen,
My time for me is irrelevant,
I am nothing but a figurine,

No one wants to talk to me,
No one wants to help me,
No one wants to be with me,
No one even wants ME,

I am but a shadow,
I have no substance for others,
I do not exist on this plane,
Astral, Ethereal, no one bothers.

Falling

Trying to do what's needed,
Blocked at every turn,
Told I'm not doing enough,
Life I want to burn,
Problems seem to surround me,
All I do is slog uphill,
Falling back more than advancing,
Never able to relax and chill,
Sleep is becoming elusive,
My time no longer my own,
Non-stop every day, all day,
I want to turn time to stone,
I need to stop and recharge,
I need some time for me,
I need to stop everything,
I need people to see,
I'm burning up everything,
I'm losing my energy,
I feel like I'm losing control,
Like I no longer have any abilities,
Noises and voices are constant,
Always inside my head,
Wall I put up are breaking,
Returning to paths I don't want to tread.

PEOPLE

My Journey- Truly

Round a sharp bend,
The train goes clickety-clack,
Oops! There goes my coffee on the floor!

A sudden slowing,
Everyone thrown forwards,
Oops! There goes my sandwich on the floor!

A surge forwards,
Momentum quickens,
Oops! There goes my juice all down my shirt!

Through a dark tunnel,
All the lights go out,
Oh bother! My magazine's gone missing!

We stop at a station,
I stand up to go,
I look out the window and see the name,
Oops! I got the wrong station again!

Through more stations,
Finally, mine,
I stand at the door ready to go,
A sudden break,
Oh, how embarrassing!!
There's me, on the floor!!!

Spirit

Where does my Spirit lie?
From whence does it come?
Invisible it is, known to our kin when we die.

What power is in thy Spirit?
What strength is in thy blood?
From what chasm did the First Spirit spring?
Who gave it right to be King?

In faith, what is a Spirit?
What use have we for it?

Spirits are what rule our hearts,
A Spirit is what drives us forth,
Allowing us to carry on,
Akin to a horse and cart.

Living in Hell

Darkness and despair,
That's all one sees when alone,
There is no guiding light,
When in a flash everyone is taken from you,

Cold and frightened,
That is all you can feel,
Fear for your loved ones,
In a room full of people,
You can be very alone,

Soldiers everywhere,
So cold, so hungry, so weak,
No hope of escape, impossible,
Faint glimmer on the horizon,
Too faint to hold onto,

Numbered like cargo,
Treated most cruelly,
Separated from friends and family,
Many of whom are never seen again,

Tired and hungry,
Irritable as hell,
Everything goes wrong,
Rations soon dwindle,
Nothing ever in ready supply,

The wireless is on non-stop,
Suddenly a news bulletin,
A sense of foreboding,
A noise overhead, Ours?
No……THEIRS,

Listening for news,
Looking for signs,
Frustrated, Hurt, Scared,
No encouragement in sight,

Sudden relief, short-lived it won't be,
Everything is over,
We've won,
We're FREE!

As I Sit

As I sit in my dark room,
I watch the rain fall outside,
I think about the warm afternoon,
Glad to be inside,

I see figures huddled up,
Others obscured by brollies,
I pick up my favourite china cup,
And think of my friend Holly,

The lamps are distorted by the rain,
The streets are filled with fog,
I look at the fire in my room,
Comforted by the sight of my dog,

As I look out the window,
I suddenly shiver with cold,
I get up and close it,
I notice the pane covered with mould,

As I sit in my dark room,
I hear laughter from below,
I smile to myself in the mirror,
And picture the happy bride and groom,

As I sit in my dark room,
I watch the rain fall outside,
I feel cold and alone, happy to be inside.

The Mission

Standing in the wings I wait,
Patiently for the show to begin,
Wondering who'll be used as bait,
Waiting for the showman to step in,

When will the fireworks start?
I watch with heavy heart,
Slowly the curtains begin to part,
The light illuminates the mark,

Imagined clapping and cheering sounds,
Surround me from all sides,
Unable to move from where I'm bound,
I watch the surreptitiously changing tide,

Slowly but surely the tide turns,
I wait breathing heavily,
To see who'll feel the burns,
The tide moves steadily,
Suddenly I hear a shout,
Jolted, like lighting, I react,
Shadows are all about,
My team appears at my back,

Triumphantly we stand together,
Our targets bound and gagged,
While our backup comes hither,
In relief we feel our shoulders sag.

Coffee World

The world goes by,
As I sit and drink my tea,
Everyone bustling and chattering,
Everything peaceful as can be,

People catching up,
On all the local gossip,
Oblivious to their surroundings,
Each giving the waitress a tip,

Their tips aren't always on money,
Though sometimes they are quite funny,
They give advice on childcare,
At every young mother, they always stare,

They often chat about fashion,
Who was wearing what,
About their fiestas,
And who did what in the parking lot!

The world passes these women by,
As they sit and chat,
Completely ignorant of their surroundings,
Too immersed in talk to watch their bags,
Nothing will happen to them though,
Everyone knows who they are,
The gossipmongers of the village,
Who sit everyday in the same, old, bar.

Who

A traveller of distant realms,
A master of time,
A man with nothing to fear,
Except his own demise,
Likes to be accompanied,
Hates to start anew,
Refuses to be still,
Despises going for the kill,
Learned in science,
Learned in languages,
Always bragging, yet,
Never truly arrogant,
Without a doubt, without hesitation,
Without a care in the world,
He puts everyone before himself,
A man with no limitations,
A man not to be trifled with,
A man not to be doubted,
A man not to be underestimated,
Under ANY circumstances,
For when he gets mad,
When he gets righteous,
There's only one thing to be done,
Bad guys must RUN!!!

The Strange Man

You find yourself suddenly in over your head,
Struggling to find your feet, wanting to be home instead,
Then HE appears, most fortuitously,
The threat is over, he makes it look so easy,

You're still scared, struggling to breathe,
Too hard to understand, he's set everybody free,
No more danger in sight, yet adrenaline lingers,
He's so full of might, constantly twiddling his fingers,

You crave adventure, he sees it in your eyes,
He gives you a choice, stay or fly?
Fly through time and space, with a virtual stranger,
Go anywhere in the universe, always facing danger,

Facing formidable enemies,
Whose hatred is fostered,
By this enigmatic character, who only
Calls himself, The Doctor.

Roofers

Drilling, Drilling, inside our heads,
Hurts, it Hurts, it needs to stop,
Somehow need to focus on work,
Before our brains begin to pop,

Sudden moments of silence,
Bring a short, inept reprieve,
Sudden start all over again,
The day we just can't believe,

Supposed to be finished already,
Supposed to be done,
Nothing seems to ever end,
We're struggling to have fun,

Drilling, Drilling, never-ending,
Hurts, it Hurts, we cannot think,
Drilling, Drilling, constant ever,
Hurts, it Hurts every time we blink!

Mr Genius

Often looks absent-minded, his eyes glassed over,
His head full of thoughts, brain in overdrive,
Always in black trousers and long-sleeved shirts,
Rarely, if ever, is he seen on the Hive,

A problem-solver, uses windows and tables,
Randomly walk in to a room full of colour and scribbles,
He's dancing around the room in excitement,
All of his movements in a constant state of wriggles,

Dry jokes, full of fun and sarcasm,
Always a half-smile on his face,
His hair gradually gets messier and messier,
The more he wriggles, wiggles and flaps in his space,

Paper piles get bigger and bigger,
With so many plates to continually spin,
He bounces around all over the place,
His face always wearing a half-absent grin.

Pippin's War at Minas Tirith

(Inspired by Peter Jackson's film)

Standing at the turn of the tide,
He waits with bated breath,
For the wave to crash and thunder,
And carry him into Darkness,

Time ticks slowly, Agonizingly by,
Whilst the World stands still,
The Silence, watchful, fearful,
With every breath of air comes chills,

Fell voices can be vaguely heard,
A murmur from the distance,
Dark shadows fill the horizon,
Fear grips the heart in that instance,

The horizon converts to swarming ants,
As the Enemy's warriors advance,
Weapons are made ready in shaking hands,
No one leaving anything to chance,

Wave upon wave come crashing down,
Adrenaline and Fear surging equally,
No notion of Time until the end,
He's standing on a field of Victory.

Thorin's Curse

(as inspired by Richard Armitage in The Hobbit: Battle of the Five Armies)

Left alone his mind begins to wander,
Unbidden, down paths that are hidden,
Seeking something that lies away yonder,
Through winding mountain passes long ridden,

Answers that his wandering need to find,
Feelings that need to be overcome,
Powers are needed to use to bind,
The seething froth before he becomes undone,

Strength, he needs to get from somewhere,
Trying to break the chains that hold it back,
Fighting, struggling hopelessly to be free,
Before falling completely into the pit so black.

Mr Legend

As cheeky a chap as can be,
Always smiling gleefully,
Ready with a joke or two,
He'll teach you to push boundaries,

Strong as an ox, as wide as one too!
He bounds down the hallways,
Don't make him angry or cross,
Because you won't be in the next day!

Loud and proud when he's in,
His presence brightens every room,
He knows exactly what he's doing,
The joy he spreads simply mushrooms!

Everyone around him starts to smile,
The banter begins to fly!
He's only ever in for a while,
His warmth, you cannot deny!

Mr Ryan

A walking work of art,
He never seems to feel the cold,
A wicked sense of humour,
His one liners are bold,

Always ready with a cheeky smile,
He'll make your lessons fun,
Dressed in a unique sense of style,
Annoy him and you're done,

He doesn't need to raise his voice,
Just speak in his baritone way,
You'll fall in line just because,
He won't let you have a say,

A tough as nails, no nonsense bloke,
A fan and extra of Dr Who,
Always walks with determination,
You'll see him in every colour but blue!

BLACKOUT POEMS

(Taken from different novels and written separately)

Stormchasers

Chapter 10, Page 87

Ella was running,
The path twisted,
She tore along,
The storm clouds racing,
Bracken flailing, sea smashing,
The wind driving her on,
Unseen presence chasing, chasing,
The cliff edge rushed closer,
The jaws of the sea opened,
She woke in the darkness.

Dracula

Chapter 3, Page 39

I was a prisoner,
A wild feeling,
My helplessness overpowered,
A rat in a trap,
I sat down quietly,
No definite conclusion,
I am being deceived,
I am in desperate straits,
The great door shut,
The Count had returned.

Frankenstein

Chapter 2, Page 27

She died calmly,
Dearest ties are rent,
The despair is exhibited,
It is so long before the mind,
But in the lapse of time,
The bitterness of grief commences,
Grief is rather an indulgence,
Is not banished,
We must continue,
To think ourselves fortunate,
The day of my departure arrived.

The amazing story of Adolphus Tips

Page 111

Mrs Blumfeld's class,
A lesson about America,
Stars on the flag,
A President instead of a King,
Great big lakes,
Great high mountains,
Prairies, deserts, and canyons,
Baseball not Cricket,
Different kinds of people,
To find freedom,
I'd like to go there one day.

The Island at the End of Everything

Page 66

We tell stories,
About an island,
Where giants live,
The ground is upside-down,
People can never sleep,
They will fall into the clouds,
A boy and a girl,
Lived together,
Made the hut,
Painting the roof blue,
Red flowers climb the walls,
Once a year the butterflies came,
Made them flicker like fire.

The Cave

Kate Mosse, Quick Reads, Page 64

The river was fast flowing,
Silver flash of fish in the stream,
River weeds shimmered,
So calm, so peaceful,
Brightness of the fields,
Shade of the wood,
No longer felt,
The presence of ghosts.

The Scarlet Letter

Chapter 4, Page 60

Return to the prison,
State of nervous excitement,
Demanding constant watchfulness,
Impossible to quell insubordination,
Introduce a physician,
Familiar with the savage people,
Much need of professional assistance,
Urgently for the child,
Writhed in the convulsions of pain,
Of the moral agony,
That individual with singular aspect,
Lodged in the prison,
Announced as Roger Chillingworth.

The Odyssey

Oxford Worlds Classics, Book XXII, Page 274

Leave this scene of slaughter,
Bard of many lays,
Anxiously peering this way and that,
Odysseus looked searchingly,
He saw the suitors,
Lying huddled in blood and dust,
"Call the nurse for me."
She stepped out, made to shout,
Odysseus checked her impulse,
"Vaunting over men slain is a monstruous thing,"
"By their own presumptuous follies,
Brought on themselves this hideous end."
"Tell me the whole truth."

MY TRIP TO SPAIN

8-2-24

Day 1

Well, the day started with a scare all right! My car battery decided that it was going to glitch this morning. This meant a phone call to the garage to have one of their guys come out to us, kick start the battery and drive to the garage so they could test it. Turns out the glove compartment needs a double click to shut fully otherwise the light stays on. A light in the glove compartment!?!?!? I never knew that! It is the only light in an automatic car that doesn't turn itself off after the engine is off. Go figure!!!

Once sorted the rest of the day went well, I finished packing all the last-minute bits and bobs, put everything in the car, said goodbye to Mum and the dog and drove to the port. Given that it was raining I gave myself plenty of time. Despite this I still managed to hit a few giant puddles that slowed me down a bit!!! Thankfully, I made it in one piece with time to spare.

Boarding was supposed to commence at 10:45 however it didn't start until 11:00 which meant we were leaving late. Once you feel those engines rumble, and the boat shudder, what a feeling!! It is so exciting! There is nothing like it! I am used to my cabin being on the same deck as the restaurants but this trip I am two decks higher up. Makes for a longer walk for breakfast, annoyingly!

Well, time for lights out! Will see what tomorrow brings in the Bay of Biscayne!

Day 2

The night went smoothly once we were out of port. The winds battered the boat rather like a boxer training with a sandbag. Everything rattled fortunately nothing rolled!

I was soon lulled to sleep by the rolling of the boat and did not wake until my alarm went off at 7am. I always like to sit where I can watch the sunrise on a boat, it is such a peaceful feeling. We were in quite choppy waters by this time as the Atlantic was not happy to see us. The sun however, rose in a beautiful yellow splendour but her shine was not to be as the clouds soon chased her away.

By mid-morning we were in calmer waters, but the clouds still persisted. The boat crew decided to do a few announcements, the first being the typical "what to do in emergency" and the second about making popcorn. The thing that made me laugh at this announcement was the fact that the crew member making it was clearly French, she had fairly good English, though her pronunciation left something to be desired. When she launched into the Spanish translation, jeez!! She could barely get the right words out!

I sat in the café during this time, writing some notes and reading a book. I was also people watching. Something I like to do. I could see people from all walks of life around me, some who had good manners and education clearly stood out from those who did not. They thought it appropriate to sit with their feet on other chairs without removing their shoes mucking about on their phones. I could see others who were engrossed in their books or their work on laptops stop to watch the sun weakly shine through the clouds for a brief moment and take photos. I could see others who were clearly uncomfortable on the boat as they kept pacing around the deck non-stop.

These people are what make the journey interesting. It is seeing how they react to the boats movement that let you know if they are frequent travellers or not. The seas have become slightly rougher since this morning. The sway of the boat is more exaggerated, and it is harder to walk without feeling yourself go with the boat!

Well, after an interesting afternoon chatting with two English couples about their lives and my life we have come to the end of the day. I do not know where the afternoon has gone! I enjoy hearing other people's stories, you can learn so many interesting things! The two couples I spoke with were opposites in that one moved to Spain and then back to the UK and the other couple have recently moved out to Spain from the UK. Neither couple are happy with the UK as it stands, and we all agreed that Spain is much more community minded in a general sense. Spanish people certainly seem to live life to the full, much more than English people it seems. However, scratch the surface anywhere and you can find so much more than you thought!

After a lovely, but expensive evening meal where I had a poached egg and asparagus to start with, followed by red lentils and chickpeas in coconut milk, with grilled mushrooms and seaweed, I now need to sort my bags out for the morning and get some sleep!

Day 3

Started with a bang! I had to get some help to kick start my battery again! Fun! Held up a few people trying to get off the ferry because of it. My phone refused to work despite having roaming on so I could not let my Mum know that we had arrived.

Then I tried to be clever and avoid the toll road that would give me the quickest journey back to my friend's house. That didn't work out and I ended up on a toll road anyway, which cost me a whopping 37 Euros! That translates to around 32 pounds. I stopped for lunch to fill up the tank and managed to get somewhere that had WIFI so I was able to call Mum. She, bless her had been frantic with worry all morning. I knew she would be which was why I video called her rather than simply send a message. I also let my friend know I was halfway to hers. She responded "okay, park near my house where you can because it's Carnaval weekend, so it will be busy." As soon as I read that I went "Damn" I had forgotten all about Carnaval.

Finally get to my friends and needless to say I followed her instructions. Tried her doorbell, she wasn't in. I wasn't really expecting her to be. I walked into town which is about a kilometre from her house. Bear in mind I have already been in the car for 8 hours at this point. I logged into the town hall WIFI and called her, she tells me she's at her mother's house. Another kilometre walk. Great. I get to her mother's house, and she isn't even there!! She has taken a disabled friend into town to watch the Carnaval procession. I have to walk another kilometre back into town to meet her. I am already exhausted by this time and beginning to physically hurt. We end up standing around for 3 hours in the cold. By ten pm I am in agony and can barely move. Time for dinner. Turns out we are eating outside because we were such a big group we didn't fit inside. Perfect!!! Sitting on a bar stool with no back support in the cold was just what I needed to end the day. Finally gone midnight we get to hers and I can get to bed. She gives me a hot water bottle for my back, and I slept like a baby.

I wonder what day 4 will bring!

Day 4

Having slept like a log I woke up feeling a lot better than when I went to bed. The day started rapidly, with having a rushed cup of tea and being told "get dressed we are going out for breakfast." I had to say I would meet them there as I was desperate for a good hot shower. I also wanted to move my car to a better parking space.

I arrive at the bar and turns out my friends husband is there with a beer, and she is at her mums. So I go to her mums, I get on really well with the family. Shortly after I arrive, her uncle and brother turn up with her nephews. Chaos!! Everybody is shouting to be heard over everyone else in their conversation, lol.

This afternoon we are going out to watch the second night of the Queens parade for the end of the Carnaval. I hope to get some good pictures tonight!

Seems I forgot about the need for an afternoon siesta! You would think I would remember that after living here for 27 years!! Hahaha. So here I am in my friend's house getting slightly chilly because she is asleep in the bedroom and her husband is asleep on the sofa with the TV on. I can't make any noise as this is disrespectful to my hosts, so I am just typing with a nice cup of tea next to me.

Well, the day ended pretty much as expected for Carnaval Queens procession. Another 4 hours standing around watching and taking photos before getting food and going home to eat. Then it was sat in bed with my friend watching TikTok videos with the heater on in her room and getting a cup of tea and going to a cold room to sleep. This is what happens when there is no central heating in the house.

Tomorrow is another day! I have some errands to run on Mums behalf so will be a day of unexpected meet and greats!!

Day 5

Different start to the day. My friend got up early for work and in her flat you can hear everything. So, she woke me up, but it did not matter as I soon went back to sleep. The next time I woke up it was around 8am. I got up and got my breakfast, then I got myself sorted, and went out. I drove back up to Sant Jordi, which is where we used to live. I thought I had dealt with all my emotions around leaving and everything that had happened whilst there. Apparently not. I broke down in tears almost as soon as I saw the church sitting on top of the hill. At least now I think I have started dealing.

Got a few of the things done for Mum, one of which was meeting with our Spanish lawyer for an ongoing issue. He was lovely and I was with him a fair while but came out feeling much better about the issue and I was able to convey that to Mum, so all good. I then went to my see my friends brother for the afternoon and we had a catch up and watched a movie. Then I watched Criminal Minds on my laptop before going to bed. So, all in all a relatively dull day hahaha.

Day 6, 7, 8

The following days consisted mostly of meeting up with people Mum and I have not seen since we left Spain. It was great to be able to have a catch-up with them all and see how they are and how they have been since we last saw each other.

It was also great to be able to have as much Spanish cuisine as I could whilst I have been here. I really do miss it. Walking along the promenade was also a nice change of pace. Everything in the UK is so fast and rushed it was lovely to be able to just saunter along and take everything in and really appreciate what I was surrounded by, which was tranquillity.

Then I saw the weather reports which were a bit alarming. So, I checked and double checked, and they got worse. I ended up booking a place to stay close to Santander. This meant that my original plan of overnight driving went out the window.

Day 9

My day started out wet, I said goodbye to my friend, had a good cry in the car before having breakfast with another old friend. I had another cry in the car after leaving him and set out on my journey north. I drove through high winds, rain, and fog. Yes! Fog! I was not able to see what little traffic there was on the road, let alone the road!!! I had to use my fog lights which is a first for me in Spain. I was in a mountain region I never normally drive in and therefore fairly high above sea level but even so, it was rather disconcerting.

The high winds left me panicked at times because it made controlling the car very difficult. Luckily that was in a flat area so no drops or sharp edges to worry about. The rain lasted most of the journey. It wasn't until I was about 3 hours away from my designated stop over that the rain stopped.

Getting to my hotel was an adventure in itself. The satnav kept telling me "Keep to the right, then turn right." Only there never was a right turning!!! Not until I got to an actual junction! Lol It took me through the back lanes which I am sure for daytime driving would have been beautifully scenic but at night made me wonder just where the hell I had booked a place to sleep! It felt like I was driving in a horror movie where I would end up at some abandoned cabin. Luckily though it was a cliff town which overlooked a beautifully picturesque landscape.

Day 10

The hotel was cheap but clean and crisp and fabulously comfortable. Breakfast was typically Spanish and fresh. The smell of coffee not so nice lol. I packed up, got everything in my car and set the satnav for the journey back out to the Ferry port.

The way out of there however was an even quicker way I could have driven in!! Turns out the satnav took me the long way round at night and the short way out this morning! I topped up the car with petrol at a local station and got on the main road. The scenery was amazing. I made good time and got to the port at around quarter past eleven am (Spanish time). Got checked in, had to open my car up and a drugs dog had a good sniff around it and got sent on my way to wait in line until we board. I will really miss Spain. It is my home and I know one day I will return to live there again. I hope soon but that will depend on circumstances.

Now sitting in the boats Lounge with a beer and a packet of crisps, I find myself with mixed emotions. I look forward to what comes next but at the same time I find myself wishing I was not leaving Spain. This has been compounded by the fact I had a Guardia Civil tell me off for not getting dual nationality!!! She got really upset that I had been in Spain as long as I had and did not take the opportunity when I had it in my hand. She told me that if I ever wanted to come back to Spain, dual nationality would have gone me through the system so much faster than without. Bless her.

Now I am back to a day and a half of terrible Tanoy announcements which hurt the ears due to extremely bad phonetics! We just got a demonstration of how to put on a lifejacket. Same as on a plane basically, bloke did not look to happy, but it was very hard to hear the lady doing the talking. She was using the Tanoy and the volume was a lot lower than the volume used for announcements.

Well, I spent most of the return trip in the cabin. I did a lot of crying over what I was leaving behind, as well as all the emotions I had squashed down. It felt good to get it all out and to start to properly let go of all my anger and resentment.

We arrived back in Portsmouth on time, got to the cars and once again mine would not start. Luckily a gentleman next to me in his camper van had a portable charger to kick start mine up. When I thanked him for his help he replied, "No problem, I got to use my new toy!"

I got home with no other issues and got sorted out and unpacked and ready to start the new week back at work!

ANECDOTES

A little taste of working in a SEN school for autistic children.

September

I did not know what to expect when I started here. It was the first time I was working with autistic children. I had no idea how hard the job would actually be. Neither was I aware of how rewarding it would also be.

These children were not happy about having their summer routines disrupted by returning to school. It took them a while to settle back into the school expectations and timetable. It required a lot of patience in order for them to feel comfortable around the new staff, so it was a month of learning.

October

Students were beginning to show their personalities and grow in confidence but were still quick to dysregulate. Half-term did not really help matters for them as it came just as they were beginning to really feel settled with everyone.

After half-term the students began to really come out of their shells, and this is when things began to get really interesting. One particular student ended up in this exchange with me after learning I am lactose and fructose intolerant:

Ss: "Here have my cheese stick."

Me: "No thank you. Why are you giving me your cheese stick."

Ss: "Because."

Ss: "Here, have my yogurt."

Me: "No, thank you but no."

Ss: "Here, have my apple."

Me: "Ss no! Thank you for the offer but I cannot eat these things. Why are you giving them to me?"

Ss: "Because I want to prove my theory! Here!" Tosses me another yogurt.

Me: "No! What on Earth is your theory?"

Ss: "I want to prove that ladies fart!"

Me: "I beg your pardon!" (laughing) "That is not a great theory."

Ss: "It's a great theory!! Here!"

Me: "No! I will not be your guinea pig!"

Ss: "You are not a guinea pig; you are a lab rat!" Tosses me the cheese stick again.

That is not the only exchange on the topic of farts for that term! This student has now lost the inclination for this theory, thankfully.

November

I started working in the school library. It needed a revamp to bring it up to scratch. Most of the books were too old and out of date so they needed to go. About 6 big boxes of books were tossed out in because they were no longer warranted. New books had been ordered and were on the way, so the remainder of the old lot needed to be sorted into their age groups.

I ended up doing a lot of time in the library sorting out and making sure the books had the school stamp on them.

I also started to get accepted by another class of students. One of them kept telling me in the corridor that *"I don't like you."*

On one particular day I asked him how he was, and he responded with:

"Not good, you are here."

Me: "Oh good! I am glad I have a positive influence over you."

Ss: "No you don't! I don't like you!"

Me: "Good. I feel really validated now, thank you!"

He started grinning as he realised that I could keep up with him. It has led now to a good relationship. He likes to be able to have a joke in class.

December

At the start of December, the school started to get ready for Christmas. Announcements went out to raise money for a local charity and sort activities for the school Christmas fayre.

Stalls went up around the school with students having competitions and selling items, mostly cakes and biscuits. It went really well with no proper upsets or tantrums; parents were able to meet staff they would not normally meet, and it was a lovely atmosphere.

We had a raffle for various prizes and the student with whom I had the exchange on farts won a prize. It was a box of bathroom pampering gear. An eye mask, bubble bath…. He turned to me and said, *"I know I've just won this, but I really want you to have it."*

I was both surprised and proud. He had managed to control his emotions and express himself clearly and concisely in a selfless manner. Something he had been struggling to achieve. I thanked him and asked him for a hug, which he gave me for a few seconds. This was another big step for him as he does not like physical contact.

Later in the school year for Mental Health Week we had a "wear it green day". I wore my old training skirt for ballroom dancing which is a lime green. I wore a pair of court shoes, which I haven't worn in a while. The student mentioned above asked me why I was wearing heels. When I responded why he said, "No offence but you have dainty legs!" I laughed and asked if he meant dainty in the normal sense of the word, his response floored me. He said, "I won't be picking you up off the floor if you fall over!"